LIFE
Chapbook

By
Stephanie Daich

Chapter 1
Emotions

MENTAL ILLNESS

Mental illness is the thing with tentacles-
That anchors in your heart-
Taking away your joy-
Ripping your soul apart-
Loneliness takes over-
As no one understands-
"Call me," people say-
With empty offers and hands-
The downhearted are left alone-
To rise above the ashes-
Even though others help-
The mental fortitude crashes-
But thankfully, after the struggle-
The light filters in-
Raise your head, fight your demons-
Let the healing begin!

LUST

Is there an emotion more powerful than you?
    You have found a way to rule the world.
    Once you have slivered your way into a human heart,
    You take over all logic and reason.
    You know how to control a human mind,
    Pushing out sanity, causing the mind to go mad,
    Forcing foolish and obsessive thoughts.
    You become the controlling emotion.
    Oh Lust, Hollywood markets you in the billions,
    Clothing lines exhort you, and ad agencies love you.
    Money is tossed your way without resistance.
    You play with the feelings and spread lies.
    Empires crumble because of your influence,
    Kingdoms walked away from, possessed by your lure.
    Because of you, families crumble and
    Educated people make fools of themselves.
    Oh, Lust, one can hardly escape your hold on this world?
    The soul has been sold in your name.
    You counterfeit love and ravish sensibility.
    Is there no way to stop your disease?

HATE

Oh, Hate, you conniving little emotion.
Thou, from whose unseen presence hearts doth die,
Spreading your black tentacles across the soul.

LOVE

adore, love
blessing from above
games, shames
love's up in flames
tease, flirt
joy then hurt
lust, passion
tender and compassion
lies, tears
exposing deepest fears
trusting, sharing
fighting then caring
reveal, hide
an emotional ride
hurting, healing
declaring personal feelings
giving, taking
loving and faking
selfish, selfless
trying to impress
tied, trapped
freedom now kidnapped
committed, invested
love often tested
peace, bliss
sweet goodnight kiss
scream, forgive
begin to live

faith, hope
wedding or elope
dream, believe
impart and receive
adore, love
blessing from above

VESSELS OF LOVE

Our bodies were designed as vessels of love,
To succor and comfort the feeble,
To give, even if we must go without.

YOU HAVE THE POWER

You have the power to choose how you are going to be.

You have the power to change humanity.

No one can make you mad or sad. Only you can create this emotion.

No one can make you succumb to their hateful or ugly notion.

When anger comes at you, block it with happiness and charm.

When anger knocks, don't let it do you harm.

You are the master of your fate. Only you can define your reaction.

You are the master of your fate. Only you can create your action.

When troubling times meet you, pull out the humor within.

When troubling times arrive, let the good define you and win.

TRUST

Trust, given freely without any guile,
Seeing the good in the person,
Using love and care to build up another.

OFFENDED

While surrendering his will to another,
While his happiness he does smother,
While filling his soul with hate,
Once in, it's hard to escape,
He ties his knots and binds his chains.
All happiness gone; only bitterness remains.
And although the slight by another, unintended.
The 'victim' chooses to remain offended.

RETURNING PEACE

A sliver of light shines through the sky,
    Brighter than it's been.
    Dark clouds overwhelming
    Drowns
    Everything within.
    Failures illuminated in shadows,
    Grinding in the sin.
    Hollow feelings spreading
    Icy,
    Jaded, forsaken.
    Killing off the happy times,
    Leaching them therein.
    Memories good are failing,
    Never
    Oh, never, again.
    Oh, but bring back the light, my strength,
    Nourishing pale skin.
    Moments sweet returning,
    Love
    Kicking in.
    Joy, pushing out the dreary thoughts,
    Incubating a grin.
    Hope, spreading as
    Good
    Feelings begin.
    Enriched by inner power,
    Defeating the grim.
    Calm and peace swelling.

Brightness,
At last, again!

STEPHANIE DAICH

LIGHT

Breaking through the clouds
Destroying all the darkness
Blessed ray of light

ABSORBED BY

Sadness, the loss of a day.
Sadness, do go away.

STUCK IN

Regrets, if only I had.
Regrets are plans that went bad.

CLING TO

Hope, look for the bright.
Hope, focus on the right.

Chapter 2
Women Issues

BEING A WOMAN ISN'T FAIR

Dear life, I don't know how to be
    With so many conflicting messages around me.
    Some say that an education will advance my career.
    Others say it depends on my boobs, hip, and rear.
    I heard true beauty is found within,
    While others define it only by skin.
    Brains are valued only to a degree,
    While most recruiters hire by what they see.
    I try not to worry about the size of my waist,
    But society makes being fat a disgrace.
    Be pretty, be skinny, be tall, thin, and lean.
    You have to be glamorous if you want to be seen.
    Can't I define who I want to be,
    Without the world degrading me?
    Can't I make strives through the talent I share?
    Being a woman isn't fair.

DOMINANCE

The prey's pheromones saturate the air.
    Ravenous wolves lick their razor-sharp teeth.
    Vulnerable, naive, so unaware is
    Their prey, as it drinks the clear spring water,
    The pack circle in, tightening.
    Wiry hair erects on the wolves' slick backs.
    -Circling closer, entrapping the prey.
    The prey looks up.
    It's too late.
    The beasts strike.
    The bottled water slips from the teen's hand.
    She is pressed squarely against her locker.
    The male team pushes harder and harder,
    Unable to restrain strong desire,
    They make their move on the loan cheerleader.
    Did she know there was danger in alone?
    Finished, they abandon her on the floor.
    -Praising each other over their cruel deed.
    Ravenous wolves lick their razor-sharp teeth.
    The smell of dominance saturates the air.

RISE, WOMAN, RISE

Within you, the grace of the universe gathers,
    A collection of positive energy flows.
    -You, a magnificent female.
    Your goodness radiates and glows.
    Why did the firmament make woman?
    -A being pure to care for the earth.
    With fierceness, yet love for another,
    To continue life through birth.
    Just like stars in heaven,
    That illuminates the dark,
    You, a mighty woman
    Rule the world and make your mark.
    You will rise above the cloudy day.
    You will lend a helping hand.
    A woman brings variety and color.
    You sprinkle hope on the land.
    So, rise, woman, above the ashes,
    You're bursting with talent and power.
    You lead with strength like a raging tiger,
    But when needed, gentle as a flower
    -Rise, woman, rise.
    You have it within.
    Your ancestors define you.
    A legacy for kin.
    -Rise, woman, rise.
    Make the most of your creation.
    Womanhood,
    a mighty station.

DEAR MAIDEN

Dear Maiden,

You try to please, always proper.

Yet your rules are impossible to follow.

You must be skinny, but not too much.

A sweet woman is what they want, but don't let them walk all over you.

To get ahead, you must assert yourself, though no one likes a Karen.

They want you to look sexy, but then they call you provocative.

They'll leave you if you don't give them what they want, but then if you do, you are easy.

A mom staying home is old-fashioned, but if you work, you neglect your kids.

They label you a feminist if you fight for your rights.

If you seek another woman, then you are confused.

You will never measure up to a man, no matter how hard you train.

If you have a high-power role, they only gave it to you because of your gender.

Dear Maiden, how can you keep up?

WARRIOR WOMAN

As they prove their worth each day,
As they fight instead of play,
As they leave the traditional role,
A position under man's control.
The warrior woman trains to fight.
Honing discipline, strong and tight.
Sweeping in, they make a place.
For the freedom we embrace.

ONLY A WOMAN AND NOTHING MORE

While on my bunk, I rested, laid out, my mind infested,
I wanted to get up and move. When do I go to war?
As I imagined, nearly dreaming, in came the light, brightly streaming.
In the light, I remembered them shutting the door, closing me behind
the door-
"Your only a woman," they muttered, "trying to go to war-
Only a woman and nothing more."
Then my anger spiked, the prejudice I disliked.
I fought the bureaucrats at home-finally allowed to join the corps.
As I trained, my muscles tightened, and feeling proud, my skills
heightened.
In my hopes, I saw me climbing, climbing up the ranks-
"Tis only a woman," they muttered, "trying to climb the ranks-
Only a woman and nothing more."
As I trained, I trained harder.
The men in my flight took rank, while to me, they closed the door.
As I watched my team deploy, I was kept on base.
On my bunk, the words repeated, repeated in my head-
"Tis only a woman," they muttered, "repeated in my head-
Only a woman and nothing more."

Chapter 3
Self Discovery

WHY MUST THE TRUE ME I CONCEAL

I show them strength
It's not real
My inner feelings
I do conceal
I laugh out loud
With lots of zeal
While deep inside
I am cold as steel
My face is painted
With lots of appeal
My outfit and style
Looks ideal
But this isn't me
This ain't real
I'm different inside
Then I reveal
They molded me
On their clay wheel
Their degradation
Is full of skill
Whenever I try to
Show the raw deal
They strongly reject me
Making me ill
I don't know how to act
Or feel
The true me
Seems surreal

Stop shunning me
What is their deal
Why must the true me
I conceal

RISE ABOVE

I need to let go of the lost dreams of yesterday.
They are not real, anchoring me to distorted lies.
This moment is real.

WHO AM I

This is what they expect of me,
    With their propaganda everywhere.
    This is who they want to see,
    When at me, they stare.
    Pre-described social ques,
    Belonging to their sect.
    Limited, closed-off views,
    That I'm supposed to perfect.
    What if there's another way,
    A different way to tread?
    They think my path does stray,
    When I do what I want instead.
    Maybe how they choose to view,
    Isn't always right.
    And even though it might be new,
    They bury it out of sight.
    Who am I supposed to be,
    When the person inside I must oppress?
    And never show the real me,
    The me, I must repress.

WHERE ARE YOU, SELF

Where are you, self? Are you in the gardens,
Stealing mom's produce, or laying on a blanket,
Watching the clouds turn into shapes?
Or are you exploring the railroad tracks,
Taking the time to have a picnic next to it in the grove?
Are you lost in an imagination that carries you
Anywhere in the world, and even outside of this realm?
What are you doing, self? Are you at a friend's,
Playing dolls and make-believe?
Have you spread out the glue and glitter while
You create the art from within?
Is that you, collecting all your loose coins from
Beneath your bed, then lugging it to the small store,
finding joy in the tiniest treat?
How do you have such a giant smile on your face with
Eyes that dance and flicker joy?
You dance and sing off-key as if you are the best.
You give yourself time to read a book and ponder its meaning.
You comfort your friend with the scaped knee
And bake cookies for your neighbors.
Then you sit among the flowers and dream of the great tomorrow.
And here you are, self, and the great tomorrow has arrived?
What have you become? Where is that fanciful folly?
You never smile anymore. Where did you leave your joy?
Many treats surround you, and yet they never satisfy.
When was the last time you looked at a cloud, imagined, created,
Dreamed, or hoped? You barely know your neighbors and rarely
see your friends.

Where did your spark go, little self?
Where are you self?

GONE ASTRAY

I lost myself,
　　As I chased a dream,
　　A dream filled with deceptive steam.
　　I deceived myself,
　　As I closed my eyes,
　　Eyes clouded by a web of lies.
　　I lied to myself,
　　As I sold my soul,
　　A soul tarnished as black as coal.
　　I tarnished myself,
　　As I gave my will,
　　A will chained to the forbidden thrill.
　　I chained myself,
　　As I lost my way.
　　A way and soul that has gone astray.

SPIRITUAL AMENDMENT

Out of the hold of the mind's deception,
    Stronger than the will of the heart,
    Spanning from thought's conception,
    The warped mental tares hope apart.
    Assessing the soul's simple pleasures,
    Harder to find each day,
    Blocking life's countermeasures,
    The desperate has gone astray.
    Pushing out the dark matter,
    Clearer the mind ascends,
    Ignoring the negative chatter,
    The lost spirit comes to amends.

ADDICTED

I took it
So I could feel
-a rush
-an explosion
-a tantalizing thrill
I continued
In order to be
-sweating
-racing
-no longer free.
I take it
It makes me glum
-dullness
-faded
-completely numb

MY SINFUL EYES

Out of my thoughts that consume me
    Untrue as a heart of lies
    I drop to a bended knee
    And cover my sinful eyes
    In the moments that define me
    I've shown my colors true
    I've set my passions free
    I've allowed my darkness through
    Beyond the settled dust
    My consequences collected
    All for a heart of lust
    My life forever affected

  STEPHANIE DAICH

FALLING DREAMS

Along the path of hope and dreams
    My inner thought loudly screams
    Of sabotage to all that's right
    To ruin all with just one night
    To break the pillars of support,
    While with deviation I cohort.
    The walls and mortar start to crumble
    When in deceit, I do stumble.
    Beholding to my thoughts, the best does fall
    Without thinking, I abandon all.
    Now all that remains is a pile of rubble
    A sickening reminder of my trouble.
    Yet, when I search the falling dreams
    Of shattered plans and broken beams
    The foundation is solidly set
    I won't abandon all just yet.

LIFE OF DISGRACE

I've done what I did.
    From my sins, I have hid.
    My staining I can't rid.
    My lies turbid.
    I took, and I stole.
    My intentions dark as coal.
    Buried myself in a hole.
    I've sold my soul.
    I can't reclaim what I've lost.
    Carelessly tossed,
    The deception does exhaust.
    Bad feelings now crossed.
    I'd ask for your grace,
    For my life of disgrace.
    But I must embrace
    My personal abase.

STEPHANIE DAICH

BAD THOUGHTS

These dreary, bad thoughts
that steal my peace and comfort.
What are they to me?
-merely a life-long friendship
Held by the king of darkness.

Chapter 4
Equality

FREEDOM WALKERS

To walk was their pride,
    Or to join a carpool ride.
    Empty the bus inside,
    The white sat mortified,
    While the black felt dignified.
    The black had been denied.
    Segregation, nationwide.
    Our own apartheid.
    Burning through the countryside.
    Black suffrage betide.
    Some felt terrified,
    As tension intensified,
    Over the bus ride.
    As races diversified,
    Buses left unoccupied.
    In court, they were tried.
    Cruelty, they testified.
    Their case bona fide.
    They had no rights; the white lied.
    Oppressed and unjustified
    11/13, change of tide.
    The Supreme Court ratified.
    Their rights certified.
    12/ 21, a new ride.
    The walkers, tears cried.
    Their dignity verified,
    Not diversified,
    No longer to walk but ride,

Most felt joy and satisfied.
Yet, some mortified
Supremacist with evil inside,
Their bombs were applied,
Trying to send hate countryside.
Some blacks sadly died.
Today peace moves worldwide.
Liberty, others supplied.
Good feelings reside,
Where human rights are applied,
Because they once walked, refusing to ride.

JAMES SMITH, THE FIRST COLORED DOCTOR

Serving at the Colored Orphan Asylum for twenty years
     And publishing medical intellect,
     An abolitionist fighting despite his fears,
     James Smith, the first black doctor, gained respect.
     Opening a pharmacy, the first African American in the nation,
     Changing the medical knowledge about race,
     Laying a vital anti-slavery station,
     James Smith promoted change with grace.
     Working with the underground railroad,
     While providing hope to a countless population,
     Much to this great man is owed,
     James Smith a man for celebration!

THERE IS A BOY INSIDE

There is a boy inside.
    He is brave as a warrior.
    He will not bow down to others
    And leave his will
    To be trampled.
    He is a champion,
    An Olympian of losers.
    He is an example
    To others equally lost.
    He can no longer wait.
    He must break free
    From the judgment and
    The scorn.
    He must present his truth.
    Will they accept?
    Will they stand by?
    Will he triumph? Or
    Will he be left alone?

FREEDOM FOR ALL IS AN ABSOLUTE MUST

An unpaid debt may be the reason why,
　They ripped husbands away while the families did cry.
　The punishment often rendered for crime,
　Was servitude that lasted a lifetime.
　A solution to prisoners of war,
　Chained humans traded and bid for.
　Owners feel superior to others.
　Some poor children could be sold by their mothers.
　Slave traders sold babies on the corner,
　Often transferred from owner to owner.
　History is full of reasons for slavery.
　Its use is society's knavery.
　Practiced in Babylon so long ago,
　Their rules were different from the ones that we know.
　Masters and slaves could be of the same race.
　To be enslaved wasn't dependent on case.
　The Romans held their slaves tight.
　Slavery brought Romes's downfall, said in hindsight.
　Farmers were removed from their land,
　Being replaced by the enslaved hand.
　The 10th century saw the Slavs subjugated.
　That's where the name of the slave was created.
　Arabs also increased the trade.
　The African people felt afraid.
　Portuguese worked to create the Slave Coast.
　Places like Seville become its trade post.
　The British jumped on the slave trading scene.
　Most enslavers were brutal and mean.

In the West Indies, sugar dominates.
Using slavery increased their estates.
America has its own darkened past.
We naively believe that slavery has passed.
Sadly today, slavery is still found.
Though often hidden underground.
Some Haitian citizens are still slaves to our sugar.
Did you know that when their islands you tour?
Disgusting is the child sex trade.
Those poor children, raped, drugged, and afraid.
How does a man raise his esteem so high?
His evil act, somehow, to justify.
How can enslavers be that inhumane,
As another's freedom, they constrain?
It's time to advocate for the good and just.
Freedom for all is an absolute must.

MALALA

Malala, you value education and advocate for it, knowing men might hurt you for your viewpoint, yet you don't back down. I don't know how your life feels. Education comes free to me. As an American woman, I can be almost anything I want. Yes, there is still oppression here in America, but we know nothing of the brutality you and your fellow sisters have gone through.

You fight for fundamental human rights. You stand and call for education. You grapple to remove the chains your society puts on your gender. I don't know how it feels to be hidden by a burqa. Here, women and little girls run around with their butt cheeks hanging out of the bottom of their shorts. All though I disagree with their clothing style, it is their right to wear what they want. I don't know what it feels like to have a garment suppress me, and I doubt neither do most of my American sisters.

Malala, you lost much in your life, and so did your people as an earthquake, wars, and a flood refaced your homeland. Then, you were taken away. It was as if they cut your knees from underneath you, yet you rose again.

Malala, you can see beyond yourself. You can sympathetically feel the oppression of the children who live in trash heaps. You advocate for them. You hurt for them. You are brave, Malala.

As you value education and essential women's rights, may I stand as courageously as you.

GOD'S GIFT FROM ABOVE

God's precious child,
Warmed hearts when she smiled.
But when the rainbow colors she donned,
All the adulations to her were gone.
Her value remains inside her,
Thou other's opinions deter.
Regardless of how she defines love,
She'll always be God's gift from above.

Chapter 5
Religion

1 in 99

The dark of night, the crying bleats.
    Far from the herd, no ears shall hear.
    On their way, the wolves make haste
    To the poor little lamb who lost its way.
    With danger drawing near, the lamb tries to hide,
    Under a log or in a bush.
    Paralyzed by fear, the lamb is unable to move.
    What is the fate of the lamb?
    But alas, when all seems lost,
    The shepherd knows the lamb's cry.
    Leaving the 99 for 1,
    The shepherd arrives just in time.
    Against his chest, he cradles the lamb tight.
    Comforted and safe,
    The shepherd brings the lamb home.

FORSAKEN SOULS

Satan, the ultimate master of disguise
Who spreads seeds of contention and confusion,
Tricking even the vitreous to forsake their soul.

GODLY TO YOU

Wild on Saturday.
Godly on Sunday.

STEPHANIE DAICH

POTLUCK

Weird food brought to the church potluck.
    Tables piled high with homemade muck.
    Last spring, twenty got sick,
    From something green and thick.
    When you eat at these buffets, you test your luck.

JUDGING

While the commandments she does follow,
    While idle sin she does not wallow,
    While taking meals to the needy,
    Even giving without being greedy.
    She holds herself on a peddle stool,
    But her religious efforts she does befool.
    Her life looks perfect without a smudge,
    Yet everyone else she does harshly judge.

WHICH IS TRUE

The bible is taught// yet translated wrong.
    Christianity is reinforced// by verse or song.
    There are many forms of God on this earth,
    Which one is true// of spiritual worth?

Chapter 6
Life

CHEMICAL BAIT

I thought I would self-medicate.
 My bosom of depression, to deflate.
 Chug down the drink, then a little more,
 Until my feelings, I no longer bore.
 My head fogged over, my senses dulled,
 A calm of falseness, I was lulled.
 My head grew tired, and my body was weak.
 Words came out mumbled when I did speak.
 All seemed foggy inside my head.
 No longer can stand, I hit the bed.
 Later upon waking, my head did spin.
 The contents in my stomach were hard to keep in.
 A vise grip seemed to crush my skull,
 Back and forth swayed vertigo.
 I could hardly rise and meet the day,
 Feeling close to death, what a dismay.
 Drinking was supposed to mend my soul,
 But I feel deeper stuck in this black hole.
 Drinking was supposed to mend my heart,
 But now, my body feels ripped apart.
 Next time I want to self-medicate,
 I will not succumb to the chemical bait.
 I'll step outside into the sun,
 Exercise, or go for a run.
 I'll take the power of what is inside,
 Instead of using a substance to numb hide.
 I'll meditate and self-reflect.
 Positive feelings I won't neglect.

I'll inventory all the good that's around.
I'll dig deep until happiness is found.
Next time I want to self-medicate,
I will not succumb to the chemical bait.

THE BEGGAR

Of me, he begs; of you, he begs.
His cardboard sign swings over his head.
GIVE ME FOOD, OR I'LL BE DEAD.

TIME

Time,

Some people squander it frivolously as if its value was nothing. They piddle it away with mind-numbing electronics, adding no value to their stature or growth to their mind. Time is more precious than metals and stones, greater than gifts of money or goods, for time provides the opportunity for anything and all.

When time passes, one can never retrieve it.

-Gone forever.

Never waste or neglect time.

Every moment is a gift to be used to the fullest.

Time, some people squander it frivolously as if its value is nothing.

OLYMPICS

As they sail across the rink,
As their bodies interlink,
As he throws her in the air,
Seemingly impossible, with much flare.
The world watches, unable to blink,
As they move perfectly in sync.
The ice-skating couple does amaze,
As the world smiles with praise.

EDUCATION

It is always good to give,
And lift a sorrowful life.
But it's better to teach,
Then just let one leech.
Education is the true gift,
When you choose to give outreach.

Chapter 7
Relationships

PEARLS BEFORE SWINE

It slipped out.
Only my heart was to know it.
But now it is out for the world to judge and see.
I have betrayed myself.
I can't get it back.
It is in the wrong hands now.
Pearls cast before swine.
Before me, my world unwinds.
Stated, its now set in stone.
Judged, tossed around by others.
Placed n the chopping block.
But it was for me to keep.
Never for others to know.

HE COMPLETES ME

It was here I first held his hand.
    The picnic spread across the grass,
    Amidst the poppies and wildflowers.
    The breeze cooled our skin
    From the heat of the sun.
    A butterfly landed on my arm, almost as if he had planned it.
    The power in his eyes called me in.
    I am here. See me.
    I drank and ate while small chatter I made,
    But there was only one thing I wanted.
    To know he felt the same spark from me.
    He gave me life.
    Everything about him is perfect,
    even his blemishes.
    He completes me.
    I can only hope I do the same for him.

BROTHER

Brother, the most glorious of words,
You bring light to my life on any dark day.
I am blessed to call you my best friend!

LET US GO

Let us go then, you and I,
When we can find the time.
Like two friends chasing an adventure.
Let us go and enjoy one another,
With conversation splendid.
Of nights beneath the skies,
And days on mountain tops.
But
I don't think you'll come with me.
I don't think we were meant to be.
∞
Let me take you past the dream,
When our hearts merge as one.
Like two friends, with years ahead.
Let us go and see the world,
With nothing holding us back,
Of nights filled with dancing.
And days blended into one.
But
I don't think you'll come with me.
I don't think we were meant to be.
∞
Let us grow old together,
When time slows down.
Like two friends, forever bound.
Let us go and forget the world,
With eyes only on the other,
Of nights spent close together,

And days by each other's side.
But
I don't think you'll come with me.
I don't think we were meant to be.

WHERE'S DADDY

"Where's daddy," his daughter cries through the night.
"Where's daddy," his precious cries at first light.
He had been there so often to tuck her in,
And always there with his morning grin.
Her face lost some of the sparkle it had,
Because she doesn't know what happened to dad.
She looks for him in the faces she does see.
But none of them are who she needs them to be.
They buried him in the ground last May.
She thought the funeral was a party to play.
She doesn't understand where her best friend went,
While the family is sad with lament.
"Where's daddy," his princess cries each day.
"Where's daddy? Why did he go away?"

ONLY IN MY DREAMS

You enter my dreams
    Every night, it seems.
    You whisk me away
    We return by day.
    Dream time is the best,
    Joined by you in rest.
    In dreams, I don't share.
    We are in love there.
    We touch, and we bond.
    You're gentle and fond.
    We travel and play.
    We're happy and gay.
    I hate when the night ends
    And you're with your friends.
    You don't know I live.
    Oh, what would I give?
    To date you for real.
    To touch and to feel.
    To have you love me,
    How great it would be.

ELECTRONIC LOVE

You made your move when you locked eyes with me at the party. You played your game. You are a player. That's what you do. I played too. That's what I do. I thought that was the end. We had fun. We went our ways.

But you texted me. You called me. -Why? There was nothing more to be gained. I stared at the phone each time you reached out, unsure what your angle was. Where were you going? It didn't make sense, but you kept connecting.

And I took the bait. Day after day, I stopped wondering why, and I started waiting, expecting those calls. I became like Pavlov's dog, salivating each time a notification came in.

Just when I started to depend on them, they slowed down, then stopped. You had become bored. That's what players do. They quickly tire of the game, but you stayed in longer than I expected. It took a moment for me to get over, for when notifications came in that weren't you, I got dry socket instead of salivating.

I have moved on.

That's what those who get played do.

LET GO OF THE STRIFE

We were young once, playing in the dirt.
We were young once when life didn't hurt.
We played in the brush and high in the tree.
We played, and we ran, our imaginations free.
There was no one in my life greater than you.
There was no one in my life I'd rather turn to.
We shared our feelings, our hopes, and dreams.
We shared our life, connected at the seams.
What happened? Where did you go?
What happened? Am I now solo?
I said a word, maybe two.
I said a word, but so did you.
Can't we forgive and let this go?
Can't we forgive? Don't let hate grow.
I need you back in my life.
I need you back. Let go of strife.
The little dispute that we had.
The little squabble made you so mad.
I told you I am sorry, every night and day.
I told you I was sorry. Can't I get you to stay?
You have been the best part of my life.
You have been the best. Please bury the strife.
We were young once, playing in the dirt.
We were young once when life didn't hurt.

BETRAYED

Betrayed by the one who should have been there.
  Discarded for a mere handful of silver.
  How could you, after all we have been through?

CHECKING YOUR HOLD

You think I am naively waiting...
  You think I am contemplating...
  You believe I am staring at the wall...
  -Just waiting for you to call...
  On the outside, I might be nice...
  But trust me, my heart turned to ice...
  I know your game...
  People like you are all the same...
  After months of no sound...
  You're just calling to see if I'm around...
  You're not concerned about my welfare...
  You're not calling because you care...
  You're only connecting now and then...
  -Making sure you still have an in...
  You want to check your hold...
  Don't bother. My heart turned cold...

Chapter 8
Getting Older

MY YOUTH HAS FLED

Oh, the youth, out me has fled,
  Leaving me almost dead.
  My mind numbs, my joints harden,
  I can hardly hear you, begging my pardon.
  I used to run, jump and play,
  Now all I do is sit and lay.
  The energy from me is zapped,
  And all I did today was napped.
  Oh, the youth, out me has fled,
  Leaving me almost dead.
  My skin was smooth and soft as silk,
  Now it looks like curdled milk.
  I used to run at the head,
  Now I get winded climbing out of bed.
  I spent countless hours playing on the floor,
  Now I can hardly walk to the door.
  Oh, the youth, out me has fled,
  Leaving me almost dead.

CRAZY AS A BAT

In the nursing home, I wander,
Sometimes fast, sometimes I saunter.
I get bored, you see,
That's when I decide who I should be.
They've closed their eyes to who's inside.
At first, it hurt, and I would hide.
But that was no way to live.
I am still full of fire, with much to give.
So, with the staff, I look for fun.
I trick and joke, and often pun.
And when they don't have time for that,
That's when I pull out 'crazy as a bat'.
I might act like a drama queen,
Demand and yell, create a scene.
Sometimes in them, I found my spouse,
And chase them around the nursing house.
Other times I'm a schoolchild,
As I run down the halls acting wild.
Once I was the God of all,
And demanded tribute as I reigned the hall.
Sometimes in the middle of the program,
I'll stand and sing and bleat like a lamb.
Once I sat in the administrator's chair,
I told him to bow and give me fanfare.
With me, they don't know what to think,
Making me visit more than one shrink.
But during those times of our private sessions,
I pull out the knowledge from my doctorate lessons.

Where the therapists see my knowledge is deeper.
We laugh, and we converse, then I'm returned to my keeper.
With a diagnosis "as smart as a whip,"
I give them a smirk, while by them, I skip.
And they are left baffled, not knowing what to do with me.
And really, the answer is quite simple, you see.
I once was a doctor, a parent, a scout,
But here, no one knows what I am about.
I ran committees, the top of my class.
Eight years in the navy earned me some brass,
But to them, all they see is wrinkles and grey hair.
They've closed off their heart without care.
I am not going to be brushed under the rug,
To be ignored and despised, not even a hug.
They will notice me. I'll make sure of that.
I am not to be brushed under their mat.
So, if they don't have time to sit and learn,
Or if they are gruff and impatient acting stern,
Then I will pull out a new character to play.
The one I will act as the entire day.
But if they want logic, then with me, take a sit.
I'll tell them my stories. It will only take a bit.
It's worth it to them, for I won't act like a loon,
Running around screaming, like a baboon.
We'll have a great visit, both will learn.
Go back and forth in respect, each taking a turn.
We should be friends, you see,
Instead of me whipping out my bag of crazy.
In the nursing home, I wander,
Sometimes fast, sometimes I saunter
If they don't pay attention to me,
That's when I decide who I should be.

GREATER THAN GOLD

A withered hand, a soggy bum,
    And wiry hairs out the nose.
    A nasal whistle, a hearing-aid hum,
    And blackened diabetic toes.
    Crevices etched deep in the face,
    And muscles that withered away.
    Little brown spots all over the place,
    And teeth hurting with decay.
    Your looks left years ago,
    Mine went ten times quicker.
    We're both old; it's so,
    As our waistlines have gotten thicker.
    Yet my love for you continues to grow,
    Despite us growing old.
    You'll always be my one true beau
    Our love is greater than gold.

SAY IT ISN'T SO

In the mirror, I gaze. // Old age I see.
    Bags and wrinkles. // Is that really me?
    What happened to my youth? // Where did it go?
    That can't be me. // Say it isn't so.

Chapter 9
Parenthood

PARENTS HOPING FOR A BRIGHTER DAY

Legs like rubber, dragging under packs,
    Backs hunched over like the aged, the youth now burdened.
    "Continue on, do not stop!" Comes the taskmaster's call.
    And onward, onward, onward, the youth are forced to crawl.
    Egos being challenged by weight too much to bear,
    Pride shedding onto the trail, the deviants brought to tears.
    "This is your last chance. It's time for you to change."
    Their parent's voices echo, echo, echo, remembering their last
exchange.
    Criminal charges pending, while academics decline,
    Addictions control their actions. The youth are forced to change.
    "The wilderness program is your last chance," they say.
    And the children are taken, taken, taken. They are taken far away.
    Trials under fire, spirits are broken fast,
    Hurdles to cross, the youth must carry on.
    "Will this program work? We can only pray."
    The parents left hoping, hoping, hoping for a brighter day.

IF ONLY I COULD STOP TIME

You step out of the changing room with a smile brighter than the desert sun, spinning in the white dress that billows around your legs.

"How do I look?" Your words send me back to years of dress-up with you strutting through the house in fancy dresses, their largeness drowning your tiny frame.

"You look gorgeous," I say, fighting the tears that threaten to spring from my eyes.

Where did the time go? Please take me away. Return me home to a simpler life-a life that evolved around picnics, tea parties, and trips to the park.

As much as I love you, you belong to your daddy. You are his girl. You two always shared a tender, special bond, a closeness I always envied, yet I melted as I watched you two together. He tries to support this significant chapter in your life, but he struggles with his breaking heart, as do I. In a month, he will give you away. He will relinquish his little girl to another man.

"How about this one?" You run your hands across the champaign satin gown. Your breathtaking beauty makes you look stunning in every dress.

Can I hold you one more time? Crawl into my lap as I rock you. Let me sing to you as you cuddle in my arms. But my arms no longer hold you at night. You gave the mantel of keeping you safe to someone else.

I delight in our closeness as we prepare for this monumental event. Can I do more to make this day perfect for you? You deserve the most elegant setting. I want to give you the world as he takes my world. But I can't forget we are gaining a marvelous son, an excellent addition to our family.

As I drive home with your dress and you return to your fiancé, I lose the fight with my tears. They cascade over my cheeks as I navigate traffic.

If only I could stop time.

DEAR CHILD

Dear Child,
Sweet child,
I wish you could see beyond the closed door,
Of the opportunities that await you.
Yes, I know the pain is real,
As you feel nothing more lies ahead.
But this is a small moment in your life.
There is so much more waiting for you,
If you will only move forward with faith.
Dear Child,
Sweet child,
Keep striving for the better.

LEAVE ME ALONE

Ambition. // Please don't bother me.
   I can't chase you. // I am not free.
   My life and time belong to another,
   Because I go by the name of mother.

MY CHILD-MY CHILD

My heartstrings cry for you.
   Don't you turn your back on me
   With language less than mild.
   My son, my son
   I've done all that I can.
   How do I instill your worth inside?
   When it's me that you shun.
   My daughter, my daughter
   You close your ears to me.
   I only hope the best your way
   As your peers, your heart, they slaughter.
   I will never understand you.
   Why am I such a bore?
   You shoot these words with nails at me.
   None of them are true.
   I loved you the moment I felt you.
   I will love you past my grave.
   You are my precious child.
   I will always love you.

THIS IS LIFE AND NOTHING MORE

Once upon daylight sadden,
    While I cried, my mind's gone madden,
    Over a life that used to be.
    Now a forgotten bore-
    While I nodded, almost dreaming
    Suddenly there came a screaming,
    From a tiny human scheming,
    Screaming outside my door.
    "'Tis the baby," I muttered,
    "Scheming behind my bedroom door.
    Only this, and nothing more.
    And the cherub babe so needy,
    Steals my time, oh how greedy.
    Change her—hold her, oh fantastic.
    Or she'll scream out like before;
    So, my life stops, to still the welling,
    I want to scream. I feel like yelling.
    With all this noise, my head is swelling.
    Dropping to my bedroom floor.
    When will she sleep? There is no telling.
    I want my life from before.
    But this is life and nothing more. But this is life and nothing more.

CHAPTER 10
RESTLESS

LALA LAND

Free at night. // My dreams weave hope.
    Shackled during the day. // Stress binds like rope.
    My burdens are hard to carry.
    I want to go to Lala land. // Where it's less scary.

TIME FOR VACATION

My next adventure calls to me,
　　To a place, I long to see.
　　Where people act a different way,
　　With what they eat and say.
　　To a region, I've never seen,
　　With oceans blue and grass lime green.
　　New smells will overwhelm my nose,
　　Of baked goods, people, and their clothes.
　　Oh, when can I leave my station?
　　It's time to start my vacation!

TRAPPED

I feel trapped. // Inside my home.
  I want to escape. // I need to roam.
  These four walls keep me closed in.
  There is no future. // Only the has-been.
  Let us run away from it all.

FLORIDA

To escape the winter and fall,
Where the heat lingers all day,
And the rolling white caps spray.
Let's go to my favorite place,
Where my petty problems erase.
Close your eyes, and you will hear,
Exotic birds far and near,
Sharing their song, beautiful and pure,
As they make their migration tour.
Feel the moisture on your skin,
Let the heat from the sun sink in.
Take a run down the private lane,
And a shower in the four-o clock rain.
At the park, see the flowers splendor,
With bright colors, delicate and tender.
We'll spend our day at the slough,
And don't forget the morning mist and dew.
Florida is my favorite location,
In North America, it's the best destination.

Chapter 11
Misfortune

THE DEADLY COST OF DESIRE

I first noticed him
From afar.
He was the tattered
Man at the bar.
His hair looked greasy,
His clothes were torn,
His face drawn out
In hideous scorn.
He had five teeth.
His smile sly,
His skin paper thin
And very dry.
What is his story?
I asked my friend.
He looks like he's
Come to his end.
My friend cautiously said,
The man's name is Jim.
He's plagued with AIDS.
Best to stay away from him.
I did my very best
To steer clear of Jim.
I avoided his gaze.
I feared to talk to him.
But one day that sick Jim
Offered to buy me a drink.
He slithered his arm over me
And casually gave me a wink.

Jim omitted a smell
That was powerfully rotten.
He smelled like something
Life and time had forgotten.
Jim said to me,
You are a lovely sight.
Come home with me
And spend the night.
I couldn't believe
He would even try.
The likes of him
With me to lie!
For starters, I wailed,
You're sick with a disease.
You're grungy, you're dirty,
And you act like a sleaze.
For your information
I am very high class.
I wouldn't even share
With you a simple glass.
You're disgusting,
You're gross, to put it quite frank.
You're putrid, you're awful,
You're downright rank.
I'd never drop down
To the likes of you.
It is something that
I would never do.
I keep my virtue
Under lock and key.
I am not that loose,
And I am not easy.

I walked away quickly
With my head held high.
I hoped Jim would vanish,
Or just up and die.
Unfortunately, Jim
Always hung around,
Quietly watching me
Without much sound.
He seemed to be waiting,
For what I didn't know.
Oh, how I wished
That he would vanish, or go.
I tried hard to ignore him,
Mingled and made new friends.
I drank, and I partied.
I followed all the current trends.
Then one great day,
To my absolute delight.
I saw my dream boat.
What a handsome sight.
I did all that I could
To snare the handsome glance,
Of this sexy new man
With the name of Lance.
He wined me and dined me.
He played his cards right.
I went home with him
Late that magical night.
My life continued on
Just like it had before.
But slowly, oh slowly,
The thief appeared at my door.

Things started changing.
I didn't feel great.
I felt sick more often,
In a horrible state.
This pattern continued
For several more years,
Until I came face to face
With my greatest of fears.
HIV, is what they said.
It is thick in your system.
There are so many in you,
It's hard not to miss them.
My world crashed hard
Around me just then.
Was this my punishment
To my sexual sin?
Things just got worse.
A new sickness each day.
My body was dying.
My life fading away.
One day at my lowest
To the clinic I went.
All of my money,
On this disease, I had spent.
I was sitting and waiting
When he walked through the door.
It was that Jim from the bar.
He looked worse than before.
Jim strode over to me
With a glimmer in his eye.
I didn't want him to see me.
I wanted to hide my face and cry.

He said, I always knew
I'd finally be with you.
Not a chance, I said.
That will never be true.
The way he looked at me
Made my blood run chill.
Through his toothless grin
He said, her name was Jill.
She was a sweet thing.
So tender and fine.
I gave AIDs to her
Right in her prime.
She became infected.
She became just like me.
She promptly spread it
To as many as three.
Lance was just one
Of those misfortunate three.
His body became indirectly
Infected by me.
You and I are
One in the same.
We both played
The deadly game.
Somehow you must have thought
You were above the disease.
You thought you were better
Than this dirty old sleaze.
You thought you were virtuous.
You made it your armor.
When you got HIV
It must have been an alarmer.

You should have known
AIDS can infect us all.
Doesn't matter if you're white,
Black, brown, short, or tall.
Your clothes could be high class,
Or shabby like mine.
Roll with the big dogs
Or druggies to dine.
You thought by avoiding me,
You could be safe and clear.
If you didn't even say hi,
You'd have nothing to fear.
But AIDS is a secret
Thief of the night.
It dampens the spirit
burns out the light.
AIDs is a nightmare,
And it doesn't care
The people it takes.
It doesn't seem fair.
AIDs breaks apart
Many families.
There's no mercy
With its causalities.
So, don't you ever put
Yourself high above me.
If you thought you couldn't get AIDs,
You lived in a fantasy.
For what is given to one
Is spread like a fire.
All for the high cost of
Fulfilling a desire.

Nothing you can do now.
The moment has passed.
The disease will be with you.
Your lot is now cast.
I looked right at Jim.
How foolish I'd been.
He was right. I'd caught the disease
Indirectly from him.
Oh, if only I could
Do it all over again.
I would stay away
From lying with men.
If only I could
Reclaim my life.
With only one man
I would be a wife.
I'd keep myself clean.
I wouldn't get around.
No AIDS in me
Would ever be found.
But sadly, I'm here
At my life's end.
Sick, dyeing, lonely,
And without a friend.
My message to all
Whoever you may be.
Stay away from causal sex and
dangerous activity.
These AIDs can infect you
Just like they got to me.
Your life will feel over.
You'll end up like me.

Also by Stephanie Daich

Alora Funk
Alora Funk - The Deliverance

Standalone
Out of Breath
Life Chapbook
Phoenix on Fire
World on Fire
Asp

Watch for more at https://stephdaich3.wixsite.com/
phoenix-z-publishing.

About the Author

Stephanie Daich sees life as a gift and opportunity for experience, discovery, and growth. She dabbles in a little bit of everything, including writing. She interacts with the world through the written word and exploration, continuously learning as much as she can cram into a twenty-four-hour period."The most significant commodity is time, and we should never waste it."

Read more at https://stephdaich3.wixsite.com/phoenix-z-publishing.